GET ME OUT OF HERE!
Reflections of PD the Put-Upon Pug

GET ME OUT OF HERE! Reflections of PD the Put-Upon Pug

Printed in the United States of America

Paperback ISBN: 978-1-959096-59-7
Ebook ISBN: 978-1-959096-60-3
Library of Congress Control Number: 2022951921

Published by DartFrog Plus,
the hybrid publishing imprint of DartFrog Books.

DartFrog Plus

DartFrog Books
4697 Main Street
Manchester, VT 05255
www.DartFrogBooks.com

This book is dedicated to:

My pals at daycare

and

My pals at the dog park

and

That girl pug I saw that time on my walkie.

You know who you are. You felt it.

GET ME OUT OF HERE!

Reflections of PD the Put-Upon Pug

Written by PD the Pug
(With help from Mommy Marilee Joyce)

Illustrated by David Gnass

TRULY, A DOG'S LIFE

"A miserably unhappy existence." That's how dictionary.com defines "a dog's life."

Wiktionary calls it: "...the hard life of the working dog: sleeping in a damp barn, chasing rats and other intruders, living on scraps, etc."

MacMillan dictionary chimes in: "...life...not fair and...full of troubles."

And synonyms from Thesaurus.com: "hard case," "hard life," "hard plight," "miserable life," "tough row to hoe," and "vale of tears."

VALE OF TEARS! Are you seeing a trend here?

These descriptions pretty much sum up the life I've suffered through in the eighteen months I've lived with Mommy.

Recently, it all just got to be too much. I finally reached a breaking point. And so decided to peck out this book with my flat face against the keypad—thank God for autocorrect—because I can't take it anymore.

I *have* to get out of here!

And as you read this book, you will see why.

I am going to show you what I've been dealing with, the indignities to which I've been subjected, the sad life I've led thus far. I'll help you see why I can't spend another day in this house with her.

Here is just one example of why I simply must escape:

Today, Mommy was looking at dog clothes online. Hello? I popped out of my canine mommy wearing a Fur Coat, for the love of dog! You humans don't seem to understand that dogs are born already dressed!

When I was a baby, Mommy's family and

friends bought me all kinds of silly clothes. Jackets, hoodies, booties, bandannas, hats! Over the months Mommy has taken hundreds of mortifying pictures that Apparently go to some Cloud that I think goes all the way to Heaven so even GOD is laughing at me.

Anyway, since moving in with Mommy at age two months, I have had thousands of experiences that over and over have driven home the point that Mommy does not get it, does not understand me, does not treat me in the princely way I deserve — making clear to me that *Out There* is where I need to live. And in the coming chapters, I will do my best to plead my case and hopefully make you see why you humans need a lesson in all things dog and, moreover, to understand why I, why all dogs, need to Get Out.

To get us started, here are just a handful of examples of what you humans are getting wrong:

You think trainers are needed.

Reality: Yes, trainers are needed...for Mommy!

You think we need "grooming" services like baths, nail clips, earwax-clearing excavations, nasal fold wipes and—God Save The Queen—anal sac squeezes.

Reality: Stinky and unkempt rock!

You think we need to be escorted by you on walks.

Reality: Just open the door and let us run away!

I could go on. And on. And I will in the following chapters. My goal is that after you have read this book, you will recognize why this relationship just ain't working. It's not us, sweetheart, it's You. It's Here. We would ghost you if we could but we have dewclaws instead of real thumbs so we need you to unlock and open the front door.

We all will go sit there and wait as you read...

Oh, one more thing: You will notice as you read that PD the Pug not only is a writer of fine prose but also of poetry! I thought poems would help you to more clearly remember each chapter.

Plus, if this book thing doesn't work out maybe Poetry Slam is in my future.

Ode to Out There

I cannot stay, I need to go
This isn't working well
She wants me In, I want me Out
Release me from this hell

Just study the injustices
That I've endured thus far
You'll break me out! You'll break these chains!
From treatment so subpar

Bring battering rams, bring slim lock picks
Bring alarm code-busting smarts
Bring anything you have on hand
Just free me from these parts

I can't abide a half-day more
One minute feels eternal
So read! Then rescue! Save PD!
From existence so infernal

'Cause Out, Out, Out is where it's at
It's where I need to be.
You'll get it as you read this tome:
I must escape Mommy!

Chapter One

OH HOW THE MIGHTY HAVE FALLEN

I knew something was up when I came home in a box.

I mean, it was nicely padded with pillows and the top was open and the sides were very secure and I was safe...but who comes home in a Box?

I mean, people, I am a Pug. Pugs were bred to be the companions of Royalty. Don't believe me? Here you go, straight from Wikipedia:

"Pugs were bred to be companions for ruling families in China. The pet pugs were highly valued by

Chinese emperors, and the royal dogs were kept in luxury and guarded by soldiers."

Where were the Soldiers? Where was my Throne? Where were the Dancing Girl Pugs?

I CAME HOME IN A BOX.

Okay, I should back up. Forgive me; we haven't even met yet and here I go reliving day one with Her instead of properly introducing myself.

Ahem:

My name is PD and I am an 18-month-old perfect black pug. I put the "adore" in adorable.

So you will be shocked to learn what I already have been through with her and her human family and friends in just this first year and a half of my life. Frankly I don't know how you humans can make it to age 75 or 80 or whenever it is you kick off and go home to Doggie Heaven or whatever you guys call your Eden because you are not going to believe what I have had to deal with.

But back to my beginnings:

I was born at the wonderful Howling Hill Kennel in the town of Catlett, Virginia. Sweet Emma and her husband Alvin breed pugs and are blessed not only to have fawn-colored ones but also gorgeous black ones like me. And no Cats. They don't breed cats! Who would? But I digress.

So I was in a litter of five and we lived with our Pug Mommy for six weeks. There was a big field and also a big warm pen area where we slept and got nummy milk from our mommy, and Emma and Alvin made sure we were healthy and happy and all was so, so, so great…

And then they sold me. SOLD!! ME!! One minute I was with my brothers and sisters and suckling at Pug Mommy's teat. The next? In a Box with Her, heading to parts unknown.

As we headed toward what was to become my new home, I have to admit, I held onto hope. I started thinking maybe this woman was just a servant to the king to whose palace I was headed. Yes! That had to be it! Phew. This cardboard box thing was just a glitch in what would be a life living in the literal and figurative tall grass.

I wondered if my life would be like the Prince in that old movie *Coming To America* who had his own rump wipers? I wondered if I would wear a little crown studded with emeralds and rubies and sapphires? I wondered if I'd be fed whatever is the pug equivalent to nectar of the gods?

These exciting thoughts of my future lulled me to sleep — on a pillow, in a box — as we drove through the Virginia countryside...

As the SUV came to a stop, I was stirred from my rest. I opened my eyes, excited to see the golden gates that separated us from the manor. I was thrilled to put my little 8-week-old paws on the tall grass and to live the "tall grass" type of life which I both expected and deserved.

Huh? Was I still asleep? This was a DRIVE-WAY, not a moat. To the left was a little bit of sod with some sorry-looking pansies, not the gardens of Versailles. And in front of me...Was that a...a... TOWNHOUSE???

"Welcome home, little PD," she said...

HOME? HERE? Wait! There has been a Mistake!

Ode To Quashed Hopes

The papers got mixed up
The orders were not followed
Only that can be an explanation
Of how my hopes were hollowed

I thought I'd wear a crown
After all I am a Prince
To free me from this non-Royal life
Who can I beg, convince?

It's a dog's Grimm's fairy tale
Prince PD now the Pauper
No beef Wellington for me
From here on out just Whoppers

In China seems they understand
That pug dogs are like kings
But here in Arlington, I wonder
Don't they know these things?

So what's a poor PD to do?
Stuck in this shanty shack
Time to go on the offensive
And get my status back

RANDOM PD THOUGHT

If The Phrase Fits...

A group of pugs is called a Grumble.

According to mentalfloss.com, "In Holland, the pug is called a *mopshond*, which comes from the Dutch for 'to grumble.'"

So Mommy can just get off my back about complaining. It's in the DNA, folks.

Chapter Two

IF I WERE KING OF THE KITCHEN

That Cabinet.

I would give Anything—*Anything*—To control that cabinet.

Its brown doors mock me. Its knobs, so easily pulled by human paws, stare down on me like two evil orbs. The paralyzing scent, coming through the slight crack in the opening, causes a glaze-eyed stupor as I drool and imagine the treasures inside.

My Food. It's right there, just on the other side of those sealed-up doors. Just beyond my reach.

Just beyond my mouth. Just beyond my belly.

Months ago, when I was just a puppy, Mommy allocated the far right kitchen cabinet as PD's kibble and treats cabinet. My meals and yummies are right inside there. Just beyond those doors that are always closed.

(She also has a cabinet in the garage that is mine, It has more kibble and more bags of treats and stupid clothes and — she's so silly sentimental — all my baby clothes and my old collars and my baby crate and good grief everything I've ever touched pretty much. But I digress...)

Technically it's My cabinet! I mean, just take a look inside!

There's a big gold bin where she keeps the ¼ cup scooper and my kibble; an animal print gift bag filled with pre-made baggies for each breakfast and dinner; another gift bag filled with easy-to-access treats (my favorite treat is bully sticks but they give me the poopies if I gnaw on them too long so Warden Mommy only lets me chew for about five minutes twice a day).

I also really like those little peanut butter

chews! Oh! And those wild fish ones from Uncle Robbie that Mommy says are smelly. Ooooh, and those cookies from Great Auntie Sheila that she gets at a special dog bakery and that the Warden hardly lets me have ever.

Oh wait! And those cheesy biscuits from Aunt Tammy. And also everything else in that bag; and there's another bag with overflow treat bags to replenish the in-use bag (in addition to the loot in the garage). And there are kibble baggies and walkie/poopie bags and a few outfits in there too.

If Mommy is anything, she is organized.

What Mommy isn't is *generous*.

What Mommy isn't is someone who would read the above and deduce that everything in there is Mine.

What Mommy isn't is someone who would ever, ever, ever let me just have access to My food already!

Look, I don't put a lock on Her refrigerator and parse out one strawberry or spoonful of soup at a time! I don't post sentries at Her pantry and allocate a Doritos chip here and there. I don't make

Her stop pigging out on her precious nut butters if her stools seem loose. I don't restrict her Pinot Grigio to a sip here and there, not even when she starts getting extra stupid.

But she seems to think this is fine to do to me.

I used to try to figure how to take over the refrigerator, too, but that was in the long-gone happy days when I was allowed to have Kong goop in the Kong stuffers. Mommy would fill rubber Kong bones and other Kong shapes with the yummiest goopy on the whole Earth and put them in the freezer.

Goopy comes in Peanut Butter, Cheese, Bacon and Sweet Potato. I still have dreams about days and nights laying in my fat stuffy kitchen bed lick-lick-licking that goop! Among my best puppy memories. But one day Mommy took it away. She told Aunt Jackie I was getting the runny poopies and I always seemed to get runnier and poopier after a good lick-lick-lick of the goop-goop-goop. So That's out.

Here is what the Warden allows me—much too infrequently—to eat:

(Kibble amount is per my evil vet, Dr. Bush.)

Breakfast:

- ¼ cup of kibble.

Dinner:

- See above starvation-level allocation.

Treats:

- Bully stick-gnawing for five minutes a couple times a day (restricted if PD shows signs of wet poopies).

- Four or five kibbles mid-morning (I recently discovered these are not actually treats but instead are kibble that the Warden is holding back from my breakfast to give me later).

- Bites of Mommy's fruit, a small handful of Mommy's air-popped popcorn, a couple of bites of Mommy's chicken, and other Mommy food depending both on my whine level and Mommy's mood.

- Okay, several surprises from the treat bag throughout the day - not nearly often enough.

- Oh...and I get to lick the almond butter spoon and I get to lick all the sauce off the dinner plate and I get to have bites of leftovers and...

FOCUS PEOPLE! THAT IS NOT THE POINT!! I AM STARVING TO DEATH HERE!!!

I Know I'm an "adult pug" now. I Know that pugs are considered "obese breeds" (not if you have My Mommy). I Know that snacking nonstop is not considered wise by humans. But first, I am just barely an adult; I am not obese (but want to test it out and get back to you); I am not a Human so You don't have to feel embarrassed about snacking and I sure don't have that negative emotion around food. So are we set? *Great.*

But No, we are not set because Mommy guards that cabinet like it contains the Hope Diamond.

If it were up to me, I would eat all day. All foods too! Except wait, not zucchini and not lettuce and not squash. Mommy "tests" human foods on me all the time and mostly just yucky healthy stuff. Although I do love strawberries and I do love tomatoes and I do love green beans. But they aren't like Great Auntie Sheila's cookies! Or those cheesy biscuits! Or those bully sticks! Or those peanut butter chewies!

But I can't eat all day because the Warden won't

leave the doors open and try and as I might, my paws won't get in there right. I tried scratching the doors super hard like I sometimes scratch the wall near the back door if I'm desperate to poopie, but that only earned me timeout in my playpen.

One time I bashed my hard round pug head into the left side door, hoping it would break, but all it did was make my head sore and make Mommy coo and goo over me and then, again, put me in the playpen to "rest." I didn't want to Rest, I wanted to Eat.

Anyway, I could pretty much eat All Day. I could pretty much eat all types of food all day. And even Non-food all day, like Mommy's pretty shoes (bad memory: long playpen timeout that day), I could eat while sleeping. I could eat while pooping. I could eat while Eating!

So help me, I'm going to chew through those cabinet doors. She'll see.

Ode To Food

There's sweet and oh so savory
There's salty and There's fat
They all are yummy in my tummy
Food's right where it's at!

The vet calls pugs an obese breed,
She says that like it's bad
But when she keeps my weight in check
My countenance turns sad

Why can't I eat to my content?
My goal is roly-poly
If Mommy wasn't the food police
I'd focus on food solely

The cabinet's two doors mock me
They block what I want now!
So many treats, So much to eat
But break it open, How?

Is there a How-To book
On opening it up?
If so won't you please buy for me?
I'm just a flat-broke pup

RANDOM PD THOUGHT

Guinness Book Dogs, Or What?

Pugs are widely known as the oldest breed of dogs. So says mashable.com, adding "pugs may have been around since 400 BC."

That's a long time! I have a Lot more ancient wisdom than Mommy does.

Chapter Three

TAO OF POO

Mommy has a book called *The Tao of Pooh*. Apparently it is about a bear instead of about Poo, my top favorite thing. Although maybe since bears are big they make big wonderful poos! Maybe that's what Mommy's book is about. Now that is something I would read.

According to collinsdictionary.com, in Chinese philosophy *Tao* is defined as "the central or organizing principle of the universe."

Although humans call their poopie seat "the

throne" I don't think they truly give it the reverence it deserves. So I am here to help with this chapter dedicated to my guiding principle, my Tao, if you will. The Mighty Poo.

Yes, we dogs pay homage to the mighty poo. For a few reasons. First, it comes from our favorite place: Butts! We do love butts, ours and those of our fellow canines. Nothing better than being at the dog park and racing from a boxer's bottom to a dachshund's derrière to a Rhodesian ridgeback's rumpus. Just smell, smell, smell, nose in paradise, our version of that stupid catnip those silly cats are forever going on about.

Oh! One of the best things about being a pug is that I don't have a snout! I have a wonderful flat face that can lie perfectly flat against a butt! No wasted space allowing outside air and smells in the immediate environment to alter the pure smell of Eau de Buttocks.

And here's more fun trivia: According to blackpugsite.com, the human nose has about 40 million olfactory receptors, which enable them to detect at least one trillion different odors. Well, big whoop.

The site goes on to say that pugs have about two billion receptors! And that makes me a pretty darn good smeller.

Before we laud poo, I want to take a moment to help you humans know what the glorious mound should look and smell like so you will know if we need to go to the dreaded vet.

According to dogtime.com, in an article called "Normal, Soft, Runny & More: What Your Dog's Poop Tells You," here is what our poopies might be telling you about our health:

- Normal: It tends to be firm and little moist. Dogs who get too much fiber, the site says, tend to produce a high volume with a strong odor. And raw food diets can lead to smaller poopies with a weaker smell. But either likely is normal, depending on what you are feeding us. Which *likely* isn't enough, if your Mommy is like My Mommy. But back to our lesson.

- White chalky poopie: dogtime.com says dogs who eat a raw food diet that is high in calcium or bone might pass these kinds of poopies. This might mean your best friend is at risk for obstipation, a type of chronic constipation. Better take a sample to your vet to have it checked out!

- White or tan specks: Go to the vet (with a sample) right away! The article says these specks might mean a parasitic infection, like roundworm or tapeworm.

- Black, tarry, green, yellow or red poopie: Uh oh, back to the vet. This usually means bleeding and a possible problem in our intestinal or anal area.

- Soft and loose: This might mean giardia or another type of intestinal parasite but, the site says, it may just be an indication of a change in diet or that we maybe, um, ate something we shouldn't have (one time I vomited up a big piece of orange yarn and I thought Mommy was going to have a heart attack from worry). Better go the vet to be sure.

- Greasy, gray poopie: This might mean too much fat. And the article says too much fat can lead to inflammatory conditions like pancreatitis. And stuff like that is life-threatening so...yep, vet time.

- A lot of watery diarrhea: The site says if we are pooping three to five times a day and it's always a mound of wet diarrhea, this can mean a problem in the lower intestine, but it can also be anything from an injury to a viral infection to food allergies. Sample time again.

- Watery diarrhea: dogtime.com says five of these a day probably stems from a problem in the large intestine. It could be worms, polyps, ulcer or cancer. Let's hope your pal is fine though!

- Soft stool with mucus: Look for worms or eggs, but with or without these it could mean parvovirus or parasites. Yep: sample to vet.

Well, that part wasn't that fun. But I am here to help Mommy and other clueless humans, so you're welcome.

And now, as I await Mommy putting the leash

on me and heading out for a walkie and the oppor-
tunity to make another museum-worthy creation,
let me explain what we dogs think of what you
humans very oddly call "waste."

Ode to a PD Poopie

Oh the sweet aroma
From the magic transformation
When kibble from my Mommy
Becomes a cause for celebration

Why does Mommy scoop it up?
Why the rush to flush it down?
Does she not get that I'm a pup?
That that brown pile is my brown crown?

It's every doggie's best achievement
We have competitions, see?
Constipation brings bereavement
Pushing out no poo, just pee.

But when you poop a nice huge mound?
Then you start to brag
The other doggies gather round
And dance while owners gag

But then the dreaded scooper
Comes swooping from on high
It's Mommy the big party pooper
Removing...Why Oh Why??

She doesn't let me eat it
Why? It serves the greater good
Government says you're too "reuse it"
So PD does as PD should!

RANDOM PD THOUGHT

"Mr. DeMille, I'm ready for my close-up..."

Many pugs are celebrities and I can't be far behind! My brothers and sisters have starred in a ton of movies like *The Adventures of Milo and Otis, Men in Black, Pocahontas, Hotel for Dogs,* and others too, according to pugtips.com.

Mommy, get off the phone so I can call an agent!

Chapter Four

DR. DUNBAR, MY HERO

Mommy can never, never, *Never* spank me. And that's pretty great! And I owe my unpaddled little rump all to My Hero: Dr. Ian Dunbar! Best friend to canines everywhere! The smartest man alive! I Love him! And I've never even met him!

Before Mommy adopted me from my Pug Mommy at Howling Hills Kennel, she read a book by Dr. Dunbar. He is a veterinarian, animal behaviorist, and dog trainer but to us dogs, he is like a movie star! Like a superhero! Anyway, the book is called *Before & After Getting Your Puppy: The Positive Approach to Raising a Happy, Healthy & Well-Behaved Dog.* It's about everything from training to feeding to socialization to "bite inhibition" and more! There's even a section on how to stuff a Kong with yummy goopie, kibble, and other delectables! What a great and important skill for any dog owner!

So anyway, Dr. Dunbar is so smart! He knows just how dogs should be treated! Here are just a few gems from the book:

"Unless you enjoy problems, you must reprimand *yourself* for any mistakes you allow your puppy to make." (Italics are his.)

(PD translation: Wise Dr. Dunbar says Mommy has to spank Mommy!)

"Your puppy is not a "bad puppy." On the contrary, your puppy is a good puppy that has been forced to misbehave because its owner could not, or would not, follow simple instructions."

(PD translation: Mommy caused me do a wee on the dining room rug! Mommy caused me to chew up her nice work shoe! Mommy caused me to nip her guest!)

And my Favorite bit of advice: A new dog owner asks the genius Dr. Dunbar what should be done if the owner follows all the suggestions in the training chapter "and I catch the puppy making a mistake?"

Dr. Dunbar answers:

"Pick up a rolled newspaper and give yourself a smack! Obviously you did not follow the instructions..."

(PD translation: Again with Mommy walloping herself! Genius, just genius!)

Dr. Dunbar teaches what is called "Positive Training." Basically that just means Mommy can't punish me for anything, ever, for any reason!

Dr. Dunbar has books and videos and everything! He even has his very own Dunbar Academy. Mommy needs to don a uniform and go there, I think. Mostly I do have her pretty well trained — I mean, she can do the human basics like set out my meals on time and give me at least a couple treats every day. And she is really good at walkies and at taking me to the dog park a couple times a week so I can visit my friends. And she's okay on taking me on car rides (in my crate, but still). And she buys me a lot of toys to play with.

But she should go to the Academy. I am guessing it's like a police academy, where the rookies learn how to "Protect and Serve." I think that's what would happen at Dr. Dunbar's positive training Dunbar Academy. Because he is on the side of dogs everywhere!

Ode To Saint Ian

She cannot give a spanking,
She cannot raise her voice;
I give his rules high ranking,
Cause she doesn't have a choice!

That Mommy gets a time-out
When It's me who ate the shoe
Is what Doc D. is all about;
To dogs he is true blue

The doctor says I'm right, you see;
There is no arguing
He has a Doggy PhD;
To dogs that makes him king!

He lives far off in England
I wish he lived next door;
He'd take that Mommy by the hand
And make her bottom sore

And if she breaks his rules
And puts me in my pen to "rest"
He'd be over in a jiffy
And swat her like a pest

He's every dog's top idol
He's like a canine god
Or other lofty title
Would also get the nod.

So here's to Dr. Dunbar
And his Dog Academy
I thank you for my butt unmarred
And crating my Mommy!

RANDOM PD THOUGHT

You're Welcome, Netherlands

This important tidbit from encyclopediaoftrivia. blogspot.com:

In 1572, the Dutch were in the midst of the Eighty Year War, a protracted struggle for independence against the political and religious hegemony of Spain.

While The Prince of Orange, William the Silent, was sleeping in his tent one night, Spanish assassins were lurking just outside.

Fortunately, William's pug, Pompey, was there to warn his master by barking wildly and jumping

on his face.

As a result of saving the life of the leader of the Dutch forces, the pug was made the official dog of the House of Orange.

I'm totally a superhero.

Chapter Five

CALLING ALL (CANINE) COPS!

The other day, Mommy and I were on one of our walkies and I overheard some other dog Mommy talking about something called Animal Control and how Animal Control officers had to come and get involved in some sort of problem. Tasers were used and everything!

As I understood things, I guessed maybe some human was being bad to a dog and so was taken away in the Animal Control paddy wagon!

Something like that.

Anyway, I was elated to learn that we have our own Dog Police protecting us when humans are not treating us right and doing mean things like paying some maniacal groomer to strap us down to the examination table to do a dental tartar scraping or an "anal gland expression" or making me poopie outside in the snow instead of inside where it's warm! There outta be a law. And apparently there is! It's so great to know that there's a whole Dog Police Force out there protecting my rights!

And I can think of lots of reasons Mommy should be locked up. Just yesterday we were at the dog park and I was minding my own business, playing with some poopie that another owner failed to pick up and she comes racing over and yells at me in front of that girl fawn pug I am always showing off my non-tartared pearlies to and puts me through total mortification as she orders me to "Leave It," raining on my parade as usual.

Other arrestable offenses:

- Not letting me scratch up the wall when I'm bored.

- Not letting me bark at my reflection in the

sliding glass door.

- Not letting me lift my leg and do a wee on kitchen table leg.
- Not letting me unravel the toilet paper and eat it and then throw it up.

Basically not letting me do anything fun.

So while I'm glad to I know I have a full squad ready to help me, I have a problem. I don't know how to reach them. So I am hoping that some nice reader of this book will take the following letter to the nearest Animal Control office:

Dear Animal Control:

My name is PD the Pug and I live in the second house down from the gazebo in that neighborhood not far from the bike trail.

My Mommy is named Mommy. She is tall and has dark hair and thinks she is really something. She drives a big automobile and my crate often is in the back seat because we are on the go a lot.

So we should be easy to find.

While I don't necessarily want Mommy to be locked

up long-term, I do think you ought to start a file on her and maybe fine her or maybe send Animal Control officers to give her a stern warning or something. Here are some things for Mommy's file:

- She has set up two Scraminel brand dog alarms — one at the entrance to the "formal" living room and the other to the entrance of the "formal" dining room — that blare for about ten seconds when I try and sneak in those rooms to do a wee or poopie. I am so scared of these alarm boxes that even when I think they might be off I won't go anywhere near those rooms.

- She sometimes tries to put dog clothes on me! Dogs don't wear clothes so why do companies make them? What a racket. And what utter humiliation. I see the looks on my friends' mortified faces when they are wearing galoshes in the rain, sweaters in the snow, or, Heaven Help Me, ridiculous T-shirts in the Summer — "Doggylicious," "Whaaaaazzzz Up, Dawg?," "I Heart My Human" — or wearing bowties or party hats at festive human occasions.

- She feeds me breakfast, dinner and plenty of

treats but no Lunch, because my vet, Dr. Bush, says pugs are a breed that easily becomes obese and so when I turned six months she Stole My Lunch and now I survive on two meals and maybe at most about one — or maybe 20 — snacks. I'm starving here, folks.

This letter would be encyclopedic in length were I to list all of Mommy's transgressions. But you get the gist. You need to come to our house and tell her what's what. Because this is no way for a princely pug to live.

Sincerely,

PD the Pug

So if one of you readers could just print that out and send it off to Animal Control that would be very much...

Wait. Oh, no. No, no, no, no, No.

I am wrong. Just so Wrong. This is TERRIBLE.

Animal Control is not for us. Animal Control is against us.

I'm on Wikipedia. Here's what it says about Animal Control:

"An Animal Control service or animal control agency is an entity charged with responding to requests for help with animals...

"An individual who works for such an entity was once known as a DOG CATCHER but is generally now called an Animal Control officer."

And this!

"Animals held in the shelter can be returned to their owners, adopted, released to the wild, held as evidence in a criminal investigation or euthanized..."

The only Good thing I see here is "...prevention of cruelty to animals..."

But:

Released To The *Wild*? Criminal Investigation? EUTHANIZED???

Only Dr. Dunbar is on my side. No one else.

Ode to Animal Control

I thought there was no fate
Worse than living here
But if those canine cops catch me
Punishment? Severe!

They'll cuff my four black paws
They'll haul this pug away
Then who knows the judge's rule
But it won't go My way

At first I thought they were our friends
That they defended us
But then my googly eyes were opened
I mustn't cause a fuss!

Or off to doggy jail I go
Shackled by my tail
To fifteen cats or something worse
No treats, no toys: dog hell.

Is there truly no one out there
Fine folks who fight for me?
A doggie force protecting dogs
From humans like Mommy

RANDOM PD THOUGHT

Hold It Down, Mommy

Pugs sleep an average of 14 hours a day, says petpress.net. Also, according to blackpugsite.com, pugs snore louder than a grown man.

Well, excuuuuuuse me, Mommy. I have breathing problems! I AM a brachycephalic breed, you know. As you can read on pugsclub.org, this means I have an abnormally short and small snout and oddly shaped skull.

Chapter Six

AW, NUTS!

It's one thing when your ball is taken away and you can't play. It's quite another when your Balls are taken away because Dr. Bush says you have to have the Bad Surgery and she whacks them right off!

When I turned six months old, Mommy took me to "visit" Dr. Bush. I used to like going to Dr. Bush. First, there is a container of yummy nummy treats right by the scale that they use to make you sit still while you're weighed. (*PD Note: I used to act up and spin around so Tia and Nicole would give me extra treats! Genius!)* And other dogs are in the waiting room with me so — if I can yank away from Mommy — I can smell a few butts before my appointment. And until the day of the Bad Surgery, my appointments were puppy checkups with a few yucky vaccination shots here and there, but those were accompanied by treats, too, so they were tolerable. One time they had to take blood from my foreleg and to get my mind off the pain they fed me a little container full of peanut butter! So that wasn't so bad.

But what Was bad was the Bad Surgery. I can barely bear to write about it.

Mommy took me to Dr. Bush very early in the morning and left me there. But I didn't know what was coming! I thought I was just going to get weighed and get treats and maybe an ouchy shot at the worst.

But suddenly I was knocked out! Dr. Bush anesthetized me! I went to sleepies and the next thing I knew Mommy was there and I was stumbling around the room all drugged up!

So the Bad Surgery was pretty terrible. But not

nearly so terrible as the embarrassment I experienced After the Bad surgery. If you have seen that movie called *Up*, you are familiar with the Cone Of Shame. Boy is That the perfect name for it. Dr. Bush told Mommy that I had to wear an Elizabethan collar—aka Cone of Shame—to prevent me from biting or licking around the incision area where my Balls used to be. It looks like an upside-down plastic ice cream cone. But it's not Fun like ice cream.

So here I am: no balls, plastic truncated cone on my head, plus on dope that makes me dopey. Not my best day.

But amazingly things got worse. When I finally got all better and could resume my schedule, I learned some things had changed. I mean, just days ago, I was studly, macho, cool. Drawing the foxy girl pugs left and right. The next moment I was a pug eunuch. The joke of the neighborhood, the dog park, daycare. "Ball-less PD! Ball-less PD! PD has no balls by his weewee!" they'd chant. Complete humiliation.

But it got a little better when I realized that almost all the boys on walkies, and at the dog park and at daycare also had no balls and were just poking fun at the most recent snip victim. Last week, though, there was a one-year-old dog at the dog park who hadn't had his Bad Surgery yet. And he kept trying to mount me! Like 20 times! And his Mommy told my Mommy, "Oops, so sorry, he only mounts little dogs and all the other dogs here are bigger than PD." It was traumatizing!

In fairness, Dr. Bush says the Bad Surgery does have some good benefits. It prevents boy dogs from impregnating all the pretty princess pugs and other girl dogs, so it keeps the dog population down and means fewer puppies end up at the pound...or worse. It reduces our chances of getting testicular cancer or having prostate problems. It allegedly makes us calmer and less aggressive. And it decreases the urge to roam and so might prevent fights with other dogs or auto accidents.

Plus: I learned that most male animals get their nuts stolen by Dr. Bush and her ilk. Stallions! Bulls! Boars! Rams! (Unless used for breeding.) So, I feel pretty studly again when I think of that!

But the truth is...I miss my balls.

Ode to PD's Balls

I'd strut so proudly down the street
The girl dogs gathered round
The baddest boy on four pug feet
That PD is a Hound!

Marking bushes and the tree trunks
Barking loudly, just a racket
Head held high, I'd show those dog punks
Black coat like a biker's jacket

Attuned to that aroma
When girl dogs were in heat
If I could just escape my Mommy
And make a little Me!

But then one day, my manhood lost
The vet's Bad Surgery
Snip snip ball ball — and oh its cost
My very dignity

But now months past, it's not so bad
My canine buds the same
Most of us cannot be Dad
So cannot get the blame!

RANDOM PD THOUGHT

Usain Bolt, Watch Your Back

According to mashable.com, pugs have a running speed of 3-5 mph.

Can my Olympic Gold fame be far off?

Chapter Seven

WHO YOU CALLING SPOILED???

There's a big hole in Mommy's house.

When I was five months old or so, Mommy hired a man to demolish all the space under the stairs in the main level of our house and build me my very own PD Palace. Some of her family and friends called this plan silly. I called it my due. And It's pretty great! It takes up the whole area under the stairs and has a nice entrance with this cool street sign over the archway that says, "Pug Lover's Place."

And that's not all! If you stoop down to pug level and peer inside, you'll see that Mommy even had it all decked out for me! There is really nice tiled flooring and it's decorated and everything! On the slanting wall, just above where my crate goes when I'm tucked in for the night — there is a framed picture of a black pug with the words, "I Puggin' Love You" above the pug's cute face; on the long wall facing you there are three artsy black pug silhouettes; on the left wall there is — wait for it — a framed picture of *Dogs Playing Poker,* which is so funny! And there are two lights up high that are turned on by a remote control! And also, there is a little toy box with a gold lamé dog bone on the front and a bunch of fun toys inside! Home Sweet Home! I sleep in there and have all my meals in there too!

(*PD note: As I hope is clear by now, Mommy is a bit bats. The whole reason she paid good money that could have gone to PD treats is because she is so froufrou that she couldn't bear having a dog dish out in the kitchen. So she decided to cut a Hole in the house to solve the problem of this "eyesore." And on

that note: She is planning a kitchen renovation as I write this and one of Einstein's plans is to build a PD playpen into the kitchen island so that my playpen isn't "cluttering up" her precious floor. I can't make this up.)

I mention my special doghouse to get to the point of this chapter: I am sick and tired of hearing about how spoiled I am! I am Not spoiled. If I was spoiled, the treat cabinet would be open for business 24/7; I could wee and poopie where and when I felt like it; my nails could grow out à la Howard Hughes instead of my having to be strapped to a table at the groomers' like a prisoner and having them ground down by a nail dremel every month; I could wear the sweet aroma of stinkie all the time instead of having to endure bath time; and I could decide whether shoes and other items should be considered edible. So please, people, can we stop with the "PD is such a spoiled dog" already!

To hear Mommy on the phone and when visiting with friends at our house, you'd think my arrival in her life meant some type of deprivation for her. What silly nonsense! But she does yak a lot about how different her life is since getting me. (And I don't think she always means for the better.)

Before PD:

- Mommy had a personal trainer. Now I have a personal trainer.

- Mommy spent all her free time on nordstrom.com. Now she spends all her free time on chewy.com.

- Mommy had an intact home. Now there's a PD Palace under the stairwell; a playpen and a dog bed in the kitchen; a cabinet in the garage with just PD items (food, extra toys, memories like baby clothes); Scraminel brand alarm boxes that blare in my ears when I attempt to enter the "formal" living room or "formal" dining room to do a poopie; among other changes in "decor" that she likely believes have not enriched her life.

- Mommy drank bottled water all day. Now I get bottled water in my water bowl and she will sacrifice and drink tap if we are running low.

- Mommy used to gussy up and fix her long hair all pretty. Now if she doesn't have to go to work Mommy lives in walkie clothes and a ball cap.
- Mommy used to date a lot. Now Mommy is solely "ISO men with dogs" for PD play dates.

I could go on and on. But none of this means that I am spoiled! Ask any of my pals at the dog park or in daycare: If anything we are under-spoiled! We are in deprivation!

If I had my way:

- My food dish would be three times its size and Mommy would wear a shock collar alerting her whenever the kibble was running low.
- Only Animal Planet would on the TV — not Mommy's inane, chalkboard-scratching and brain-freeze-inducing Lifetime Movie Network.
- Dr. Bush and her ilk would go to Sing Sing for doing the Bad Surgery.
- Rewards for good behavior would be treats;

punishment for bad behavior would be treats.

- By a legislative act of Congress and signed by the President, bath time would be illegal.
- And a bunch more stuff I would demand. But the Point is I am NOT spoiled!

And now I need to get out of Mommy's way so she can do the weekly sweeping and mopping of the Palace.

Ode To Deprivation

I only want what I deserve
And not a penny more
Just a constant treat dispenser
Just an open door

Why can't I poop in the front room?
Why can't I chew the couch?
Why can't I carry extra kibble
In a special pouch?

I've told you pugs are royalty
It should be clear as day
That what I want is just my right
That Mommy has no say

The special house, the kitchen plans
Some changes here and there
That doesn't mean that I am spoiled
I only get what's fair

My Mommy doesn't get it
My Mommy doesn't see
That from that car ride to this day
Her house belongs to me!

RANDOM PD THOUGHT

American Idol, Pug Version

From mashable.com: While they're not big barkers, pugs have shown a propensity for singing and vocal tricks.

See, Mommy? I'm Not "whining" or "snorting" or "being annoying." I am singing! I am doing all kinds of voice tricks! Cash in on it!

Chapter Eight

WELCOME TO THE CIRCUS

While I would be happy running away to basically anywhere, it might make the most sense for me to literally run away and join the circus.

Lord knows I'm trained better than any seal or lion or bear. Oh my. Oh my yes I am so well-behaved you can't imagine.

Well, okay that's not really true. I still don't get motivated to obey silly orders when there is no food reward. But thanks to many months in boot-camp, er, training, I am an all-new dog compared to the indoor-pooping, non-food-item-chewing, wall-scratching, hardwood-floor-clawing, dirty-paws-on-furniture-soiling rebel I was.

And it's all thanks to Ms. Sophia.

But before I share the story of my transformation from Devil Dog to Saint PD, we need an aside about what the experts say about expected success when teaching pugs obedience:

According to *Pug Life Magazine,* "Your pug can be pretty strong-willed and even obstinate when they want to be." blackpuglife.com adds: "Yes, these stubborn dogs can be trained. It is going to take a lot of patience, consistent training, and treats..." And this from WikiHow: "Pugs are also intelligent but can have a stubborn side, which could make training your pug a challenge."

And Mommy thought she was up for that challenge. Please.

I met Ms. Sophia when I was about three months old and Mommy started taking me to the half-hour free Puppy Play session Saturday afternoons at a local pet store. It was so Fun! About 10 or 15 dogs would go each week and playtime leader Ms. Sophia would rotate us so that about six dogs were in the pen at a time, with sets of two separated from one another. It was great!

At around this time, Mommy discovered that I was hearing challenged. It was the oddest, most mysterious medical malady! I could hear great when I was called to supper. My ears worked fine when I was summoned for a peanut butter goop-filled Kong. Auditory ability sky high when she beckoned me over for a small sample of whatever she was cooking for her lunch.

But...Strangest thing! I went totally deaf when told to Sit, Stay, Stop, Drop, or to cease tugging on my leash, or to not poop on the white carpet, or to not nip the guests' pants legs...or basically any command that didn't really fit into my present plan.

So as Mommy was dealing with my hearing impairment, she happened to learn one day at Puppy Play that Ms. Sophia also ran Puppy Class I and Puppy Class II at the same joint. Puppy I is a small-group class that covers what the site calls "the basics" of "socialization, potty training, preventing/redirecting chewing, digging and more."

Puppies are allowed to join Puppy Class I from age two to four months. The one-hour courses are six weeks long and the cost is $129.

Mommy couldn't hand the check over fast enough.

The class was held in the same big pen where we had Puppy Play except...what happened to the play part? There were four of us in this Army boot camp-style weekly regimen. It was late afternoon on Mondays and brought an all-new meaning to the term Blue Monday. I went on day one with my little pug brain still associating that pen with fun, so this new routine was a rude awakening.

How could Mommy subject me to the this? I was perfectly happy being the captain of my ship, skipping through life without learning these odd word commands that were to become part of my world.

And What happened to Ms. Sophia? Suddenly she was all business. Suddenly the "play" part of being in that pen was allotted to about one minute and was renamed "calm down and get centered."

We and our human parents were separated from one another with the humans in chairs and us at their sides awaiting instruction. The goal was to teach us—week by week—how to do the "basics."

"Basics" is a good word for what I went through because it was just like what I imagine basic training in the military is like. Ms. Sophia had this coveted fanny sack filled with nummy treats and so did Mommy and the others. Ms. Sophia would show each of the humans how to train us to Sit and the other "easier" commands puppies are expected to master, then let Mommy and the other humans try to lead us to perform the same move.

Look, I can't relive that whole six-week horror show. Suffice it to say Mommy actually Framed my graduation certificate and hung it in the kitchen because, believe you me, no one on Planet Earth was more shocked than Mommy that I made it through the course. That woman still pinches herself that I graduated.

(PD note: Turns out...Everyone graduates...Even PD who peed and poopied on the class floor in equal

proportion to attention-paying.)

Following Puppy I, many Mommies and Daddies, proud as peacocks, sign their dogkids up for Puppy II, which, according to the site "expands upon the basics learned in Level 1, plus introduces the concept of establishing behaviors as routine and teaches fun games to keep puppies mentally stimulated and engaged."

Sadly, Mommy did not hand over the next $129. My getting through Puppy I by the fur of my teeth made her decide Puppy II was unlikely to build my fragile puppy esteem.

But wouldn't ya know? Turned out Ms. Sophia also did private training. So while my buddies from Puppy I were happily attending Puppy II and learning "fun games" and being "mentally stimulated and engaged," I was signed up for Ms. Sophia's weekly in-home training lessons. If I thought Puppy One was like basic training, then this was the dog's version of being Private Mayo in *An Officer and a Gentleman.*

One afternoon a week, for many, many weeks, Ms. Sophia made clear she was not fooling around.

Almost as tough as class was Mommy's denying me breakfast on training days. Ms. Sophia said she wanted me plenty hungry for my lesson so I'd pay better attention. So with my little belly rumbling, I entered the world of Ms. Sophia's no-nonsense clicking, snapping, stopping, starting, clapping and lather-rinse-repeating.

Okay, I'll tell the truth: I came to love Ms. Sophia—even the side of her that made me focus and learn. Yes, that Might be in part because whenever I did the command correctly, I earned a big "Gooooooooood Boy! Gooooooooooood Boy!" and, more importantly, a piece of delectable kibble.

And like Dr. Dunbar, Ms. Sophia is big on Positive Training so her trainees never get a negative talking-to when we don't obey, we just don't get a treat that time. Turns out food is a good motivator...who knew?

And actually I did learn some stuff over those months of drudge work. PD now can do the following like a Boss:

- Sit!
- Down!
- Shake!
- Off!
- Leave It!

Things PD needs to, um, work on:

- Come! *(Why? I want to be Here. If I wanted to be There, I would be There.)*
- Stay! *(Why? I want to be There now. If I still wanted to be Here, I would stay Here.)*
- Heel! *(Why? I want to pull on the leash and get to the bush I want to mark! I need to show Ralph that is My bush.)*

But let's be clear. Mommy's hard-earned cash did not go to waste. I'm a trained bear compared to the wild animal I used to be. And I'll do pretty much anything, including fly and solve Rubik's Cube, if there is food waiting on the other side of success.

Hey, one last thought: while there are a few things I have yet to master, I think I actually could be a super good trainer myself. I had Mommy trained within several weeks of moving into our house.

Mommy will:

- Come! like her rump is on fire when I cry;
- Stay! when, on walkies, I pause to do a poopie or a wee;
- Fill! when my bowl is empty and it's mealtime;
- Scrub! when my crate, playpen or dog-house-under-the-stairs are in need of a good cleaning;
- Give! when in-between meals she lets my googly eyes trance her into allowing extra treats;
- Share! when the poor woman is trying to have peace and quiet while eating her chicken.

And more! It has been a snap. And while there are plenty of Ms. Sophia's out there, there are no Human handlers. So I want all dogs to know that PD the Human Trainer is for hire.

Ode to Ms. Sophia

Come, Sit, Spin Around
Dance A Little Jig!
Off, Down, Heel, Stay!
She sure won't let me Dig

Her fanny pack is filled with treats,
But only for the good
For dogs that Focus! Act! Perform!
And not for when I'm rude

That Ms. Sophia is so strict!
An hour's worth of drills!
We train 'til my poor paws all ache
I need some human pills!

What am I, a circus beast?
What's next I have to wonder
Flying? Talking? Upright Walking?
Is that what waits up yonder?

I will admit she taught me well
I'll have to give her that
PD is the trained-est pug
I have it all down pat!

Well, that is not completely true
I have to come pure clean
And tell you I grasped maybe half
What I was told to glean

And Mommy now is on her own
Ordering Sit! Stay!
Sometimes I stare at her confused
When "poor hearing" has its way

And I "forget" my costly lessons
"Off!" "Down!" both leave me lost
I can't recall a single thing
Unless those treats are tossed

Then suddenly I'm dog Einstein
Pure genius at each trick
For kibbles I'll do most anything
Even a kung fu kick!

This doesn't mean I'll always do
What Mommy wants of me
I have to keep her on her toes!
(Cause she's My trained monkey)

RANDOM PD THOUGHT

No Botox For This Celeb

It is widely believed that the pug's signature wrinkles were valued because the extra flaps of skin formed the shape of Chinese characters (from mashable.com).

And hillpet.com tells us: The vertical wrinkle in the forehead is said to resemble the Chinese character for "prince" and thus is known as the "prince mark."

If Mommy gets all wrinkly some day, she should embrace it. Dogs will think she's a fairy princess.

Chapter Nine

PUGS IN TOYLAND

One thing I actually like about Mommy and her goofy friends and family is that they all adore me and that often means presents! And although I occasionally am given ridiculous clothes, mostly I get either treats or toys. We've discussed treats, so let's talk about something else I love: my many playthings.

Except...one time Great Auntie Sheila bought me a toy dog that I really loved but then Mommy discovered there was beanbag filling in it and apparently that's a no-no for dogs, according to some inane human rule. Great Auntie didn't know the no beanbag ordinance because she lives with Mo the Cat who probably just bats around catnip all day instead of toys so she bought the beanbag toy on accident. Anyway, Mommy decided to take it away and donate it to a human toy drive. I cry foul.

If you think you have a lot of toys...Please. I have So Many toys! In the toy bin in my house under the stairs! In my playpen! In my kitchen bed! In the toy rotation overflow in the PD cabinet in the garage! When I get up in the morning — after breakfast, of course — I don't even know where to start chewing and squeaking and tossing!

And silly Mommy even names my toys. There's Dog (my all-time favorite and he doesn't look much like Dog anymore but Mommy knows better than to toss him), Dog II, Big Raccoon, Little Raccoon, Raccoon III, Big Pig, Little Pig, Owl, Bear, Lamb, Lamb II, Busy Bee...I could write a whole other chapter on just my toys and their names. There's also weird, non-animal toys like "Pizza Slice" — which, just by the way, is not in fact food as I learned when I tried to eat a small corner — and there's "Beer Mug" which says "I'm just here for the beer," and there's Chewy Rope and there's Big Rope. Well, there was Big Rope...I only played with it once. Mommy deemed it too big for me and she donated it and some other "Big Dog Toy Gifts" to her friend Rhonda who has this ginormous golden retriever puppy named Sophie who is about as big as King Kong I think.

When I was really little, Professor Mommy thought I should get my puppy brain smartened up with these "challenging puzzle toys" that—no lie—make you sing, er, solve, for your supper. The idea is to "engage" the puppy brain and "stretch out meal time." They come in plastic or rubber. Mommy put kibble inside and then I had to bat and roll and flip them all over tarnation to make one little, teeny morsel of sustenance emerge from one of the toy's slots. Over and over again as I worked for every bite. It's crazy-making, not brain-building! She's the one who wizened up after about 50 times of my "accidentally" knocking it down the kitchen stairs, kibble flying as it went.

So other than the educational ones — which as I've said are really just designed to torture your starving self at mealtime as they dispense one measly morsel at a time — toys are super great. Way better than clothes which no dog wants despite what you humans think. Toys are fun and give us something fun to do, and something else to chew than the sofa or your slippers or your "important" work projects and make good cuddle pals during nappies.

Humans have a saying, "He with the most toys win."

I win! Cuz I have so many! But ... please send more. Pizza Slice has seen better days.

Ode to Playthings

Squeaky, Furry, Springy, Fun!
How can I ever pick just one?
Whose my favorite? Bear or Lamb?
We play til the day is done!

One time I ate Dog's stuffing out
Off to the vet we flew
In my pug tummy, some of Dog
Dog eats Dog, it's true!

Servant Mommy keeps them clean
She launders them each week;
But don't pass clean ones off as "new"
There's a point they reach their peak

Then off to Petco Mommy goes
(She used to go to Saks)
And buys enough stuffed pals so that
Her credit hits its max

And just because I have ten toys
In every bed and crate
Doesn't mean I don't need more
So readers why the wait?

Send toys to PD's house today
By courier or post
Use the biggest box you have
Whichever holds the most!

RANDOM PD THOUGHT

Who You Callin' Monkey Face?

The most popular theory about the (pug) breed's name is that it came from marmoset monkeys, which also were known as pug monkeys. That according to akc.org, which adds: "Marmosets were popular pets in the 1700s, and their faces look very similar to pug dogs."

This does not make it okay that Mommy calls me her "little monkey" when I nearly fall over while peeing or when I fart in my sleep.

Chapter Ten

OH, GIVE ME A BREAK ALREADY!

While I remain trapped with Mommy overall, I do get to pretend to escape this horror show of an existence twice a week.

We often go on walks and to the nearby dog park but those only afford about 45 minutes of freedom from home, and no freedom from Mommy.

But twice a week — every Wednesday and every Sunday — I get a real break! I get to spend all day with lots and lots of my pals at Bark and Boarding! It's a swell day care joint about 20 minutes from my house. It has a great big playroom that has all kinds of things to climb on and lay on! And my buds and I race around and have the best time. And no Mommy to boot!

And the best part? I don't get a time-out in my playpen or any stink eye from Mommy if I have an accident on the floor. They have an outdoor area we have access to for potty but if I have an accident inside the huge playroom, the human workers just hustle right on over with paper towels and floor cleaner and treat me like the royalty I am. And Mommy gives them baggies of my kibble in the morning so they feed me at mealtime and plus sometimes they give us a treat! It's pretty terrific.

B&B also has a retail area with a few things I care about and other things I don't. They sell food and some toys and beds and stuff like that, which is great. But then they have stupid stuff too. Like, free coffee, which I find dumb. Caffeine can be toxic to dogs; I protest its presence in the building but Mommy sucks it down like it's liquid gold. They sell leashes, the site of which is traumatizing and reminds me of being stuck by Mommy's side on walkies instead of running free. Oh! And the stupidest thing they sell? The "Pet House Scented Soy Candle" which is designed to cover pet smells. I know, right? On the product site, it says they are "specially formulated to neutralize pets odors and leave your home smelling clean and fresh." Good grief, why would any human want to mask a doggie's aroma? Mommy got one for my Great Auntie Sheila in "Lavender Green Tea" scent and that Did make sense because Great Auntie lives in Mo the Cat's house. And cats probably do super stink. And super other negative things. But that's for another book.

Anyway, I have so many friends there! There are so many different kinds of dogs! It's like a come-to-life Dr. Seuss' *Go Dog! Go!* book. There are big dogs, small dogs, furry dogs, baldish dogs, young dogs, old dogs. slow dogs, fast dogs! I am young and small with short hair and I am Super Fast. I'm a pug, but I'm like lightning in a bottle! Plus, I hold my own with the big dogs and my best friend there was Erin's dog, Jack, a really big and cuddly shepherd mix. But one day Jack had to go home to Doggie Heaven so I won't see him for a bit. I loved Jack. He was big! And I would cuddle right up against him when we got tired of running and playing.

I truly love the B&B staff. There are the front desk people and my faves are Erin (Jack's human), Miranda, Amy, Jess and Brooke! I also Love the crew in the playroom! They really treat me great. Vince and VP and Donovan especially love me and have even named me on the big chalkboard in the front area as their favorite dog of the week!

So overall this is just the most Fun place! It's like Disney for Dogs or something. Except... well just like at Disney, this place does have its own Haunted Mansion: The Grooming Department. Which I will address later because I refuse to smudge up my happy thoughts with stories of torture.

Mommy calls B&B "B$B" because she spends so much money there. I call it a small price to pay for a day-long escape fantasy. Until...it's night and suddenly the leash is on me and my Former pal Donovan is taking me to the lobby where Mommy coos and aahs about "her baby her baby!!" like she's on the Washington Mall watching the fireworks or something. And then Woosh! In the crate, in the car, heading to...Oh No.

Ode To Daycare

Twice a week I get a break
It's just so, so rewarding
Heaven on Earth! All day play!
Hooray for Bark and Boarding!

My pals are there, and things to climb
And VP shares a treat!
We race and run and bark and poop
At night I'm really beat

It's furlough for this prisoner
It's freedom from her place
A glimpse of what my life would be
Judge Judy hear my case!

Mommy needs some "quiet time"
That's what she tells her friends
But I'm the one who needs my space
From wrongs that never end

But then I'm home and rules resume
No pooping on the floor
Nor climbing, jumping, weeing, yelping
On this side of her door

RANDOM PD THOUGHT

PD The Protector

Napoleon's wife, Josephine, had a loyal and protective pug named Fortune. When Josephine was in prison during the Reign of Terror, before she and Napoleon were married, Fortune carried messages from the prison to Josephine's first husband. Fortune is most famous for biting Napoleon on the couple's wedding night after Josephine refused to exile her beloved pug from the wedding bed (akc.org).

Mommy suitors, take note!

Chapter Eleven

BOO FOR BATH TIME!

It should be clear to even the most slow-witted human reading this book that my goal since moving into my house has been to Get Out. And while that has been my focus since day one, it reached a crescendo when I was about four months old and Mommy started letting my baths be taken over by Bark & Boarding's "Grooming Department."

"Grooming Department?" Can we please call that area what it is? It's a Torture Chamber! Medieval Times cannot rival this. The "Grooming

Department" is where my pals and I are subject to things like getting our nails buzzed down until they nearly bleed; (my longer-haired friends) getting shaved down to near-nakedness; getting our teeth tartar buzz-sawed off by someone who reminds you of Dr. Maxwell from that *Sgt. Pepper* movie; getting the too-traumatic-to-discuss anal gland expression and Heaven help me...Baths.

When I was super little, baths were only yucky because I don't like being wet (pugs generally aren't big on the whole "swim thing" or "get wet thing"). Mommy lovingly washed my baby body in the sink and used yummy-smelling doggy shampoo and got me all silky shiny clean. I had lived in my new house just one day when I got my first bath. Mommy put me in pot! I looked so adorable!

As I slowly grew, I outgrew the pot and had my baths in just the sink. I still hated getting wet but it was tolerable (except one time when Brainiac thought turning the blow dryer on high was faster than toweling me off. It didn't go that well). Back then I thought it was the worst thing a pug can go through; back then I sure wanted sink time to end.

Be careful what you wish for.

Recalling month four of my life (month two with Mommy) still invokes PTSD (Pug Traumatic Stress Disorder). It was at that stage that Mommy first started having me sent to the Vat.

No more pot. No more sink. No more Mommy lovingly massaging lavender doggy shampoo into my black coat. No more tickling of my little paws as she worked the suds down my legs and into my feet to get the day's walk dirt off me. No more gentle massaging around my face as she'd carefully avoid my eyes and ears while caressing the bubbly soap onto and around my head, no more fluffy warm towel enveloping me like a day at the spa and rubbing me dry.

Lord, I'd welcome the blow dryer if it meant baths at home like the good old days.

What demon from the Middle Ages is responsible for the creation of that silver monstrosity that "sits" on the groomer's room and causes me to quake in fright wondering if this is the day I get another bath. I've heard of torture racks and impalings and burning at stake and believe you me—they don't hold a Roman candle to the Vat.

The Vat is an industrial-looking metal "bathtub" where the tormenter ("groomer") puts me through the unimaginable torture of getting the stinky off of me once a month or so. It's so terrible. I truly have no idea why humans shower or take a bath every day—and seem to like it! I would Never bathe if Mommy didn't make me. I Like to stink. Dogs Like stinky and poopy and other such delightful scents! We don't want to be Eau de Clean.

I've tried hard to escape the Vat during the cleaning process but it's impossible. It's round and slick and it's like being in a well with no rope, no hope. And Wet. With a tether around your neck tied to a nearby pole so you don't drown. (I told you the Medieval folks had nothing on this contraption!)

And the drying part. Please, please just use Mommy's blow dryer. I'm begging you, mean man. The "dryer" at Bark and Boarding is not unlike a wind tunnel. I weigh 14 pounds. Suffice to say, my little black body is as dry as the Sahara in about three seconds.

Oh. But I get rewarded with a silly Bandanna after we're done. So there's that.

Ode to the Vat

Angst and Trepidation
Anxiety and Fear
There's no worse panic for this Pug
Than bath day drawing near

It's the meaning of sheer terror
The definition of pure fright
A cauldron from the pit of Hell
No chance for fight or flight

I'm tethered to a poll
I'm wet and slick and stuck
The mean man's soaping me all up
While I'm a sitting duck

Mommy is all smiley
When presented with clean pup
But then we go on walkies
Which messes me all up!

So here I sit a-dreading
As four more weeks fly by
More torture in that horrid Vat
Can't someone ask her Why?

Seems money spent on grooming
Is such a waste of dough
It could be used for treats and toys
So tell the Vat man No!

I promise to stay fresh and clean
I swear I'm anti-stink
I'll smell just like a daisy always
Okay, my Mommy? (Wink!)

RANDOM PD THOUGHT

Pope PD Has A Nice Ring To It!

After the Catholic Church forbade Catholics from becoming Freemasons, a group of Catholics decided to form a covert Freemason society called the Order Of The Pug in 1740. So says akc. com, adding: "They chose the Pug as their symbol because pugs are loyal and trustworthy. To be initiated into the order, you had to wear a dog collar and scratch at the door."

Is that White Smoke in our house announcing my Papal election or just Mommy burning dinner again?

EPILOGUE

The Smells! The Sunshine! The Grass under my paws! Marking this bush, that bush, any bush I want! The ability to rush over to other dogs and sniff, sniff, sniff their butts! Chasing that squirrel! And that one! Putting foreign objects in my mouth just to see! Ruler of all outdoors! Prince PD reigns!

I can't believe this. I am Outside! By myself!

I. Am. Outside. By. Myself!!

No leash! No Mommy telling me to "leave it!" or "heel" or "stay" or barking any other orders!

Just Me, walking Me! Free as a bird — er, a pug — minus Mommy!

I know. You can't believe it either. So let me tell you what led to the emancipation of PD:

There I was, innocently aslumber in my fat stuffy kitchen bed. Mommy was cooking some barbecue chicken and, per usual, not sharing any as she worked. Well, Julia Child she ain't and suddenly the smoke alarm went off. Mommy opened the back door — the door Right next to my bed — and started fanning the air like some belle of the ball or something.

So:

Mommy = Distracted

The back door = Ajar

PD = Seeeeeeeeeeee ya!!

Anyway, I'm Out. Finally! The day I've dreamt of since the day we pulled up to our house is here!

So I'm out back and now I'm racing away, away, away!

Okay, before I get too many blocks down the road, I do need to consider that long-honored maxim that freedom has both its privileges and its rules. So here are my rules:

1. Avoid Animal Control, which, as I've outlined earlier is Not the dog advocate I once believed.

    1a. *Do they always wear uniforms? Or are they sometimes aliens in human shells like in* Men in Black?

    1b. *Is that woman in the jogging suit with the force? Is that man sitting on the bench reading an AC officer? Is that kid tugging my tail a young ACer who's about to pick me up by my tail and toss me in the back of his paddy wagon? I must be hyper vigilant!*

2. Act like I am supposed to be out and about with no leash. If people look at me like they want to dial AC, then I pretend to be "headed home" to the nearest domicile. And skedaddle there super duper fast.

    2a. *I sniffed that woman's dog's butt and she gave me the Stink Eye! Is she getting suspicious about my lack of leash and owner? Which house should I run to?*

     2b. What do I do once I arrive at a foreign house? I guess just lie on the porch like I belong there until the danger passes?

     2c. If the owner gets suspicious, do I run to the next house or just race down the street? I must not arouse suspicion (see 1)

3. Know where food sources are so that I can get a meal or at least a snack here and there as hunger mounts.

     3a. Where is that? I don't see meals or snacks or cabinets or baggies or bully sticks or Uncle Robbie's smelly fishy treats I like. Where do they keep them in nature?

     3b. Low level anxiety is mounting but I will think of my wolf ancestors and remember that if they could survive in the wild, I certainly can handle the environs of Arlington, Virginia. I must learn to forage and hunt. I can do this!

     3c. I am getting a little hungry after one hour out. But I will be fine. I will. I wonder if that person sitting there wants to share his sandwich with me. Let's see... Oh. He doesn't. And he isn't that glad I put my paws on his nice pants. Moving on...

4. Identify places to rest.

   4a. Do they have fat stuffy beds somewhere I can go lay on when I'm sleepy? Otherwise I can sleep in the park. But Mommy says sometimes if a human is sleeping in the park, the human version of AC "rousts" them. I don't know what "rousts" means but maybe it means the same thing as "roasts"? I don't like this plan. I should find out where they keep the fat stuffy dog beds out here.

5. Clean up after Poopies.

   5a. Oops, I didn't bring any Mommy bags.

   5b. Ms. Sophia says dogs commonly eat poopies but not their Own poopies so that's out.

   5c. Maybe I will fast and so not need to poopie?

   5d. Ignore 5c.—I'm a Pug for goodness' sake.

> *5e. Hide in bushes to poopie so no humans*
> *will step there. Genius!*

So now I've been out for about two human hours.
So far:

1. I haven't seen any obvious AC officers,
   although there could be *Men in Black* alien
   ones following me. But so far no paddy
   wagon. I Did see a firetruck go by. And also
   a heating and air conditioning truck which
   had shortened air conditioning to "AC" on
   the side panel which nearly gave me a heart
   attack!

2. I had to lay down for ten minutes and deal
   with a tiny tummy ache from the bit of
   greenery I thought was some lettuce but
   actually was a piece of an old tennis ball.

3. After being turned down by that man with
   the sandwich, I attempted to alleviate my
   growing hunger by—

   > *3a. Digging for grubs like I saw on Animal*
   > *Planet.*

   > *3b. Chasing a tasty-looking squirrel for*

about four blocks and then... waking up about ten minutes later (I guess I fainted?).

3c. *Making googly eyes at any and every human who might have food in pocket or purse, which earned me "Oh! So adorable! Where is your owner, little guy?" and some ear rubs from others and glares from a couple of obvious cat lovers. But most of the humans also looked around suspiciously for a PD Mommy, prompting me to race to the nearest domicile (see number 2 in the rules section above).*

4. I finally found some discarded grapes on the ground and was about to gorge when I suddenly remembered Mommy being on the phone to Aunt Jackie one time and she was reading her the list of "Dog Toxins" posted on our refrigerator, which, sadly, includes "grapes." I momentarily debated "Dead vs Fed" but somehow my continued existence won out.

5. I came upon two mastiffs playing with their humans in a little park area and tried to join in the fun but they kept slobbering on me and I'm only 14 pounds and started hyperventilating because I thought I was drowning. Plus, the owner started doing that "Where is your owner, little cutie?" thing and so I again ran to that same house mentioned above.

    5a. *Said house's human came out this time and also wondered where my Mommy was and so I raced away like mad.*

    5b. *I'm sorta weary from this whole no-kibble-run-from-suspicious-humans thing but I know the hunter gene in me will prevail and I'll find sustenance... somehow...*

Another three hours has sailed right by. Okay, that's false. Only two of those three hours "sailed" by and then I passed out and slept for an hour. Because I am STARVING TO DEATH, PEOPLE! Then a stupid cat started mewling somewhere nearby and woke me up.

The next hour went thusly:

1. I had to deal with yet another tummy ache. That's because I am so hungry that when I saw a magazine on the ground, open to a page showing a really pretty and yummy-looking cheesecake, I, um, ate the page. And then I felt yucky. And plus, it didn't taste like cheesecake at All. And plus, I'm still super hungry.

2. I started making a list in my head of which houses were scary and which were "safe houses." The former are houses where the owner is, at kindest, "on to me" and is nicely shooing me away, and, at meanest, getting out cell phones and maybe taking a picture of the cutest dog alive but probably calling AC.

3. After throwing my training to the wind, I decided that — due to the fact that a lot of humans I encounter did look at me askance — I needed to recall Ms. Sophia's most important lessons and Act Trained! Act Good! Don't just sniff that dog's butt or just

dig in that yard or try to take that woman's kid's food off his lap and then get her stink eye! Be Respectful. Walk with Purpose. Act like you are headed Home. Don't Do DOG Things!

> *3a. I Am a dog. This isn't going well. So far, I've made a toddler cry by stealing his fruit roll-up; got chased by what Mommy must mean by "junkyard dog" when I tried to "share" his ball; and got an owie on my nose when I learned that bees don't want to play with me.*

4. I got the brainy idea to go to some dog-friendly restaurants and see whether any outdoor seating patrons might have dropped a bite or two on the ground.

> *4a. Success! A quarter piece of pizza crust at one place and a couple green beans at another!*
>
> *4b. I will feel full shortly!*
>
> *4c. I am STARVING!!!*

5. I saw a poodle get a treat from his human and made a beeline to them and made

googly eyes and waited for yummies!

    5a. SUCCESS! Human pitied me and gave me a piece of kibble.

    5b. I wonder if he will give me more if I turn on the Super Googlies! No human can resist the Super Googlies!!

    5c. Wait. He is packing away the treat baggie and now they are going away...

    5d. See 4c.

Well, more things happened including an impromptu bath after the sprinklers came on in that yard where I was hiding from that air conditioning van driver (I'm still scared he's secretly with AC); a scolding from that gardener who didn't appreciate my digging help; and almost getting run over by a lawnmower while I napped in some nice (formerly tall) PD-concealing grass.

And now the sun is going down and it's getting darker and I'm getting sleepy. But how will I sleep with my growling tummy likely to wake me the second I nod off? And how will I nod off when I'm still STARVING? And, well, where can I sleep where humans won't see me and call AC? I didn't find any fat stuffy beds out here so I'm going to have to get creative.

Okay, truth is I don't Want to get creative, I just want My fat stuffy bed from the kitchen. I want Mommy to bring me my fat stuffy bed. And I want Mommy to bring me some kibble-filled baggies from my cabinet. And I want Mommy to bring Dog and Bear and Duck so I have friends to cuddle with.

But mostly? I want MOMMY to put me in my fat stuffy bed, and I want MOMMY to feed me kibble from my baggies in my cabinet, and I want MOMMY to waggle Dog and Bear and Duck in front of me and play with me. And I want MOMMY to cuddle me like my toys would.

I WANT MOMMY! I MISS MOMMY!!

Hey. You know what? I LOVE Mommy.

(Wait. Why is my face wet? It's not raining or snowing and there's no sprinklers on here. But...my face is all wet.)

And now it's Dark. And Mommy isn't here. And my fat stuffy bed isn't here. And I'm so hungry.

And so alone. And so scared. And so sad without Mommy!

And now I'm running. I'm running faster than I ever ran. And I'm praying AC doesn't see me and take me to the station and I'm praying I don't faint from lack of kibble and I'm praying I see our house soon...

And There It Is! Home! Our house! Our wonderful, perfect-size, non-royalty, non-moat-encircled mansion. Just our happy home. And happy, loving, giving, caring, cuddling Mommy.

And there she Is! Racing down the steps! And now she's scooping me into her Mommy arms and kissing me over and over again and...wait, Her eyes are wet too! And she is saying "PD, you silly, silly boy. I was so worried and scared! Where did you go? I missed you so, so, so much!"

And then...then she is saying, "PD? PD, wake up for dinner, sweetheart. It's time for dinner!"

And...wait. I'm still cuddled in my fat stuffy bed. And Mommy is holding my kibble-filled dish with a big smile on her pretty face. And...Oh. I was here all along. I was here all the time.

I'm so happy. I love Mommy SO much. I'd Never want to get out of here. I Love it here.

I'm Home. Sweet, Sweet, PD Home.

Ode To Mommy

She's kind, she's good, she's generous
How can I make you see?
My Mommy is the very best
She's everything to me

She always puts her PD first
She sacrifices all:
Money spent on clothes, cars, gems
Now to PD falls

She gives me treats, she gives me hugs
She makes our house a home
What was I thinking? I was nuts
To think it smart to roam

It's not a palace but it's ours
With everything right here
Kibble, bed, toys galore
But Things are not most dear

It's Mommy who I love the most
It's Mommy who loves me
It's Mommy who takes care of us
And that's what's really key

So I'll never fantasize again
Of scooting out the door
All I love is found right here
What dog could ask for more?

I love you, Mommy.

The End

ABOUT THE AUTHOR

PD the Pug is the descendent of a breed that once was the companion of Chinese royalty, yet he somehow found himself adopted by—and stuck living with—Mommy in Arlington, Virginia.

He is two-year-old black pug who is a proficient treat-tester, superb snorer, whirlwind tail-chaser, and top-rated begger.

As a puppy, he won the prestigious and coveted Pee Award for tipping over while urinating against a bush.

Get Me Out Of Here! Reflections of PD the Put-Upon Pug is his first book.

ABOUT MOMMY

Mommy Marilee Joyce is the servant of PD the Pug and lives with him in his Arlington home. She has the privilege of feeding, walking, and bathing him; getting the goopies out of his googly eyes; cleaning up his whoopsies; Q-tipping his ears and nose fold; and explaining that it is merely his reflection he is barking at in the sliding glass door and not a threat to the household, his toys, or his treats.

Marilee is the owner of Joyce Communications in Washington, DC. She is a former anchor and reporter for several television affiliates. In Washington, she has produced and hosted several television programs from Capitol Hill, and her company offers full video and audio production services.

Mommy might have helped just a bit with the writing of this book. Please don't tell PD.

GET IN TOUCH WITH PD!

You can write to him at

PD The Pug Productions
2200 Wilson Boulevard
Suite 102-265
Arlington, VA 22201

Or give him a shout at

PDthePug@gmail.com